AF584431

World Heritage Sites in Australia

Sydney Opera House, Gondwana Rainforests, Blue Mountains and more...

New South Wales

Ellen Millen

First published 2017 by
Redback Publishing
PO Box 357 Frenchs Forest NSW 2086
Australia

978-1-925630-15-2

Author: Ellen Millen
Editor: Jane Hinchey
Designer: Redback Publishing

Original illustrations © Redback Publishing 2017
Originated by Redback Publishing

Printed and bound in China by Leo Paper

Acknowledgements
Abbreviations: l—left, r—right, b—bottom, t—top, c—centre, m—middle
We would like to thank the following for permission to reproduce photographs: (Images © shutterstock) p5b Hung Chung Chih, p16b GagliardiImages, p17 Aleksandar Todorovic, p22tr Lucie Lang, p24br By Stephen Gard - Own work, CC BY-SA 4.0, https://commons.wikimedia.org/w/index.php?curid=53309357, p24b By Stephen Gard (Own work) [CC BY-SA 4.0 (http://creativecommons.org/licenses/by-sa/4.0)], via Wikimedia Commons, p25b By Stephen Gard (Own work) [CC BY-SA 4.0 (http://creativecommons.org/licenses/by-sa/4.0)], via Wikimedia Commons,

Every effort has been made to contact copyright holders of any material reproduced in this book. Any omissions will be rectified in subsequent printings if notice is given to the publisher.

Contents

Page 6 World Heritage Sites and UNESCO
Page 9 Sustainability and World Heritage Sites
Page 10 Heritage Organisations in Australia
Page 14 Gondwana Rainforests of Australia
Page 16 Sydney Opera House
Page 18 Australian Convict Sites
Page 26 Willandra Lakes
Page 28 Greater Blue Mountains
Page 30 Lord Howe Island Group
Page 32 Glossary
Page 32 Index

What Makes a Place Special?

All around the world, people show that they value special places in different ways. Sites that are special because of their history, beauty or spiritual significance are preserved so that they do not deteriorate and will still exist for future generations to enjoy. Special places can be important for just one person, a group or community, or for everyone in the world.

Various groups in communities look after their special places in different ways

UNESCO

UNESCO identifies World Heritage places around the world.

Governments

Governments at all three levels in Australia make laws and regulations to identify, preserve and protect special places.

Community Groups

People in a local area often join together in groups to protect special places from destruction. Protest groups in Australia have been successful in the past in helping to preserve places of natural and built heritage. Many people donate their time and skills to help maintain special places such as bushland sites or historic buildings.

Individuals

Individuals who care about special places can look after them by being careful not to do anything that might degrade a site. Avoiding littering, not lighting campfires in the bush on days of high fire danger, and not engaging in graffiti or other unlawful activities all help to preserve special places.

Special Places

Make your own list of special places. The list could include homes, shops, parks or even a room or a special spot underneath a tree.

- Why are these places special to you?
- Will they still be important to you in the future?
- Are your special places important to anyone else?

Think about the places that are important just for you. Are they the same places that your friends or family think are special? What makes a place special to you?

World Heritage Sites and UNESCO

UNESCO is a division of the United Nations. It assesses sites around the world for their cultural and natural value to humanity. In 2017, there were 1,052 World Heritage Sites worldwide. Nineteen of these are in Australia.

> *"To be included on the World Heritage List, sites must be of outstanding universal value and meet at least one out of ten selection criteria"*

World Heritage Convention

The work on cataloguing World Heritage Sites began in 1972 as a result of an international treaty known as the World Heritage Convention. Australia was one of the first nations to become involved. Once a World Heritage Site has been determined, the country in which it exists must preserve and protect that site. Countries which have signed the treaty can work together to preserve sites that are of international importance.

World Heritage Committee

The World Heritage Committee is a group of some of the member countries of the United Nations. Committee members serve a fixed term. The role of this committee is to administer all matters relating to World Heritage Sites listings. Australia has been a committee member on a number of occasions.

UNESCO's World Heritage Mission

- To encourage more countries to sign the World Heritage Convention and contribute sites.
- To encourage countries to set up management plans for their sites.
- To provide emergency and technical assistance.
- To encourage local populations to become involved in preserving sites.

Threats to UNESCO World Heritage Sites

World Heritage Sites that are in danger of destruction are listed by UNESCO in their List of World Heritage in Danger. None of the sites in Australia are currently on this list. This is due to the diligent work undertaken by governments and individuals in Australia, and the high regard that Australians have for their heritage sites.

Threats to sites on the List of World Heritage in Danger currently include:

- Natural disasters like earthquakes or cyclones
- Wars and civil conflict
- Uncontrolled expansion of towns and cities
- Unchecked tourist development
- Neglect
- Lack of funds
- Pollution
- Poaching

In 2017, there were 55 sites listed by UNESCO as being under threat.

Historic Centre of Rome, Italy

Ha Long Bay, Vietnam

World Heritage Fund

Member nations contribute to the World Heritage Fund. Countries that do not have the financial resources to care for a site can apply for funding to assist them.

Notre Dame Cathedral at Reims, France

Saving World Heritage Sites

UNESCO has been involved in saving some of the world's most iconic sites and their surroundings, including:

- Angkor, Cambodia
- Dubrovnik, Croatia
- Giza Pyramids, Egypt
- Delphi, Greece
- Abu Simbel, Egypt
- Venice, Italy

Old Town of Lijiang, China

What is a Plan of Action?

Before setting out to protect a heritage site, it is important to have a Plan of Action. This plan will help to make the conservation process efficient and therefore more effective. Whether the heritage site or special place is being cared for by a government, a community group or an individual, their Plan of Action can include the following points:

- Set a definite goal.
- List the things that may stop this goal being achieved. Examples are a lack of funds, unfavourable weather or groups which oppose the goal.
- List all the activities that will be required to achieve the goal.
- Set priorities for which activities are the most important.
- Decide who will do the work required to achieve the goal.
- How will the goal affect other people who are not involved?
- Where will the funding come from?
- Work out a timetable for achieving the goal.
- Have regular reviews of the Plan of Action and make changes to it if necessary.

How a Heritage Listing Affects Communities

When a place receives a heritage listing, either from UNESCO, a government body or a private organisation, the listing can result in both positive and negative impacts on the community.

Positive Effects

- The heritage site is preserved for future generations.
- Owners of heritage listed buildings can apply for grants to help maintain them.
- Nations can apply for funding from UNESCO to care for their World Heritage Sites.
- More people know that the site exists.
- The world community can encourage nations to continue preserving their sites.
- Heritage sites produce a positive economic effect through their impact on tourism.

Negative Effects

- Indigenous people living in the area may be stopped from using it as a food source and as a place to perform traditional ceremonies.
- People may be stopped from using land as a holiday campsite.
- People cannot usually take pets with them into natural heritage areas.
- Farmers who have been grazing livestock in an area may be stopped from doing this.
- Houses that receive a heritage listing cannot be demolished or changed. Owners need special permits for any work on their building.
- Access to some areas in natural heritage sites may be restricted.
- The construction of roads and buildings is either not allowed or restricted.

Sustainable Tourism in World Heritage Sites

Tourism is a significant activity in World Heritage Sites. UNESCO advises countries with World Heritage Sites on sustainable ways to manage tourism.

At Australian World Heritage Sites, sustainable management of tourism includes:

- Building boardwalks or raised viewing platforms in natural areas so that tourists do not damage the environment when walking through it
- Closing sites, allowing them to regenerate
- Controlling the provision of sewerage and garbage services
- Restricting or forbidding access to sensitive areas
- Banning pets
- Educating the public on the value of the sites and how to behave when visiting them

Sustainability and World Heritage Sites

- Natural sites are involved in carbon storage in the form of trees and plants.
- Natural sites contribute to the water cycle and to climate regulation.
- Natural sites contribute to maintaining the Earth's biodiversity. This is important for the health of humanity, since many of our new medicines come from research undertaken into the properties of rare plants.
- UNESCO reports that climate change is likely to affect World Heritage Sites.

Q&A

Q. Can a place ever stop being a World Heritage Site?

A. Yes. The Arabian Oryx Sanctuary in Oman and the Elbe Valley in Dresden are no longer listed after failing to meet the requirements for preservation of the sites.

Stromatolites in Shark Bay

Heritage Organisations in Australia

The Role of Governments and Heritage Councils

UNESCO is not the only organisation that determines whether places have heritage significance. The three levels of government in Australia, federal, state and local, also compile their own listings of important places. There are many more sites and items on these lists than on the World Heritage List for Australian places. Each state and territory has a Heritage Council which advises government on matters relating to heritage places.

Historic Shipwrecks Program

Shipwrecks more than 75 years old are protected by legislation. No items can be taken from them and divers must not move any part of the ship. Severe penalties apply. Shipwrecks that contain the remains of people, unexploded ammunition on warships or other sensitive contents may have access to them restricted. Anyone who discovers an historic shipwreck must report it to the government department responsible for shipwrecks in the relevant state.

Famous Australian Shipwrecks

- HMS Sirius in Slaughter Bay, Norfolk Island is one of the ships of the First Fleet
- Japanese midget submarine M24 from the Second World War is in the sea off Sydney

Overseas Special Places For Australia Listing

This listing is created by the Australian government.

- ANZAC Cove, Gallipoli
- Kokoda Track, Papua New Guinea
- Howard Florey's Laboratory, Sir William Dunn School of Pathology, UK

National Trust

The National Trust has organisations in each state and territory. Their aim is to preserve and promote Australia's cultural heritage. The National Trusts own over 300 heritage places.

Australian Institute of Architects

The Australian Institute of Architects keeps a list of notable buildings of cultural heritage across Australia. A building's importance is based on its aesthetic, historic, social, spiritual or technical value to the community.

Heritage Homework

Some school buildings around Australia are listed on state heritage registers. Is your school one of them? Are there any heritage listed school buildings in your area?

Shipwreck
ANZAC Cove

Australia's 19 World Heritage Properties (2017)

1. Australian Convict Sites
2. Australian Fossil Mammal Sites (Riversleigh / Naracoorte)
3. Fraser Island
4. Gondwana Rainforests of Australia
5. Great Barrier Reef
6. Greater Blue Mountains Area
7. Heard and McDonald Islands
8. Kakadu National Park
9. Lord Howe Island Group
10. Macquarie Island
11. Ningaloo Coast
12. Purnululu National Park
13. Royal Exhibition Building and Carlton Gardens
14. Shark Bay, Western Australia
15. Sydney Opera House
16. Tasmanian Wilderness
17. Uluru-Kata Tjuta National Park
18. Wet Tropics of Queensland
19. Willandra Lakes Region

Gondwana Rainforest

All World Heritage Sites in Australia are protected by law under the Environment Protection and Biodiversity Conservation Act 1999.

Sydney Opera House

Kata Tjuta National Park

Jim Jim Falls, Kakadu

Gondwana Rainforests of Australia

These sub-tropical rainforests are located in the southeast of Queensland and the northeast of New South Wales. They were first listed as a combined World Heritage site in 1986. Millions of years ago, rainforests such as these covered most of Australia. Some of the plants and trees found in the rainforests are direct descendants of ones that once grew on the ancient continent of Gondwana. The rainforests are a world repository of very precious vegetation, such as the descendants of ancient ferns, conifers and primitive flowering plants. These plants are only seen as fossils elsewhere in the world.

History of European Settlement in the Gondwana Rainforests

- Early settlers cleared rainforests to provide land for farming and housing.
- Roads and railways were built through the rainforests so that miners and farmers could transport their products to ports and markets in large towns.
- Rainforest trees were logged for their timber.

Threats to the Gondwana Rainforests

- The World Heritage listed areas that form the Gondwana Rainforests are not all connected and some are not very large. This makes their management difficult as the habitat for the plants and animals in the smaller parts is restricted
- Climate change
- Uncontrolled tourism
- Bushfires
- Feral animals

Sydney Opera House

The Sydney Opera House has been a World Heritage Site since 2007. It has a unique design that inspires architects around the world. The shape of the building refers to shells and sails, both deriving from its harbourside location near the Sydney Harbour Bridge. The white exterior is covered in interlocking glazed tiles and the large expanses of glass allow panoramic views of the harbour from inside the building.

Designed by Danish architect Jorn Utzon, the Sydney Opera House was built amidst controversy and arguments about the cost, the time taken and the way the internal spaces should be used. Jorn Utzon resigned in protest and other architects completed the work. Queen Elizabeth II opened the building in 1973.

History of the Site

Located at the place where the first colony in Australia was founded in 1788, the Sydney Opera House is iconic in every way. Its outstanding design, use of original engineering solutions for the construction, and the unparalleled historic location all make the Sydney Opera House one of the most important public buildings in Australia.

The Opera House is located on the land of the Gadigal Aboriginal people. It sits on Bennelong Point, which is named after an Aboriginal man who was an important figure in the early colony. His hut was located on the land. In later years, Bennelong Point became a tram depot.

The Sydney Opera House and Sustainability

In 2015, the Sydney Opera House became one of the few heritage buildings in the world to win an award for its efficient use of energy. The cool interior during Sydney's sweltering summers is achieved using a special cooling system installed underneath the building. Maintaining a steady temperature is very important for the many musical instruments used in the Sydney Opera House.

Heat Exchange System

The Sydney Opera House uses complex technology called a Heat Exchange System to cool the interiors. This technology utilises the seawater of Sydney Harbour. Most visitors do not realise that there is an unseen engineering marvel beneath the beautiful white shells and the public spaces of the Sydney Opera House.

Did You Know?

Part of the funding to build the Sydney Opera House came from a lottery run by the government.

Australian Convict Sites

Why Are the Convict Sites Important?

Australia was founded as a convict colony, a place where Britain could send its thousands of prisoners. Convicted for a variety of crimes, including theft, assault or causing political disturbances, the convicts provided the labour which allowed Australia to grow into a bustling colony of Britain. They included women, men and children from the age of nine years old. The last convicts arrived in 1868, ending 80 years of transportation. Australia has eleven early convict World Heritage Sites.

What Do the Convict Sites Reveal About the Past?

- The types of housing people lived in.
- The difference in housing and places of work of different classes of people.
- The harshness of the punishments for criminals.
- Many jobs that once existed are now replaced by technological inventions.
- Technology has replaced domestic animals in transport and for ploughing fields.
- The daily life of convicts' children was very different from that of children today.
- We can observe how some building methods have not changed very much at all.

1. Old Government House, Parramatta, NSW

Old Government House is the oldest public building in mainland Australia that is still standing. It replaced the first government house in Sydney and was the home of the governors and an administration centre for the early colony from 1788 to 1856. The building sits in Parramatta Park, which was once called the Government Domain. Once the trees were cleared from the Domain, it was used for agriculture and keeping domestic animals. Old Government House was constructed on the lands of the Dharug (Darug) Aboriginal people.

How is the Site Maintained?

Old Government House has been carefully restored and is now a house museum that is open to the public. The style of the furnishings and the collection of household implements are displayed to make it appear that the house is still in use by unseen governors, servants and convict workers. Visitors can imagine themselves living in the colonial era, using kitchen tools that did not depend on electricity. They can also see for themselves the differences between the way the governor and his family lived and the way the convict labourers were accommodated.

The surrounding Domain is a public park but still has the remains of a number of outbuildings, including the dairy, ornate gatehouse, bath house and astronomical observatory.

What Are the Threats to the Site?

The historic site shares its location with a recreation space for thousands of people from densely populated areas surrounding it. Parramatta Park is the venue for large events, including New Year's Eve fireworks.

2. Hyde Park Barracks, Sydney, NSW

How is the Site Maintained?

The first government barracks built for male convicts are located in the centre of Sydney and are now restored and used as a museum. The barracks show visitors where the convicts lived after a hard day working in the chain gangs around Sydney, and where they slept in swinging hammocks. Before the sturdy barracks were constructed, many of the convicts lived in tents or huts. Some were able to take on extra work for themselves and could pay for a room in a hotel. The new barracks resulted in them being much more strictly controlled by their guards.

Convicts were not the only people Britain sent to the colony of New South Wales. In the years 1848 to 1850, over 2,000 Irish orphaned girls arrived, some of them no more than fourteen years old. The Hyde Park Barracks had ceased being a home for male prisoners by this time, so the girls were sent to the barracks to be housed and protected from the dangers of trying to find accommodation for themselves.

The building was designed by the convict architect, Francis Greenway. Governor Macquarie ordered the construction of many public buildings and he often used the skills of the convict population. He was criticised for this by his superiors in Britain who thought he was spending too much money in the colony and allowing convicts more freedom and rights than they deserved.

Demolition Threats

Although the Hyde Park Barracks are now a preserved World Heritage Site, they were under threat of demolition a number of times in the past. As the city of Sydney grew around them, the barracks were once considered ugly and worthless. Due to the work of people interested in the conservation of Australia's built heritage, the Hyde Park Barracks have become a site of world importance.

What would you have done?

Francis Greenway was an architect in England, before being transported to Australia for forgery.

Apart from Hyde Park Barracks, Francis Greenway designed many famous Australian buildings. Can you name three?

Do you think Governor Macquarie made the right decision letting Francis Greenway work as an architect?

3. Cockatoo Island, Sydney Harbour, NSW

Cockatoo Island is the largest island in Sydney Harbour. From the 1840s, it was used to house convicts and separate them from the main settlement. Cockatoo Island was meant to be a place of severe punishment for convicts who had committed further crimes after arriving in the colony.

What is Preserved?

Buildings from the convict era include a convict barracks, hospital, mess hall, guardhouse, military living quarters, and Biloela House, the original superintendent's house. The convicts quarried stone on the island to build Fitzroy Dock, which was the largest public work anywhere in the colony at that time, and is now the oldest surviving dry dock in Australia. The old machinery left after decades of shipbuilding make Cockatoo Island an important place for research into Australia's industrial archaeology.

Child Prisoners

In 1869, the island was formally separated into two sections. One section served as a prison and the other as a dockyard for ships. In the late 1800s, inmates on the island included girls under sixteen years old who had committed crimes, and boys who were orphans or homeless. Cockatoo Island gives visitors today an insight into the way these young people were treated, whether they were convicted criminals or not.

Shipbuilding

After the prison was closed, the whole island developed into Australia's main shipbuilding site. It was a naval dockyard during both World Wars in the 20th century.

Wheat Silos

A drought in the 1830s led the colonial government to order the construction of huge underground storage silos for wheat. These wheat silos were built by convicts who cut the bottle-shaped pits out of the sandstone.

Tourism

Cockatoo Island is now a place where tourists can go to find out about colonial convict history. It is also used as a venue for cultural and music events. As with many other heritage sites in Australia, tourism plays a vital role in helping to fund maintenance and in spreading information about the historic value of the location.

Bushranger Escapes!
Captain Thunderbolt, the notorious bushranger, and his accomplice, Frederick Britten, managed to escape from Cockatoo Island in 1863.

4. Old Great North Road, near Wiseman's Ferry, NSW

The Old Great North Road is significant because large sections of it look nearly the same as they did when convicts finished working on it in 1836. Today, people can study the road-building techniques of that time and also imagine the harsh work conditions experienced by the convict road gangs.

Why was the Road Constructed?

Building of the Old Great North Road began in 1826 and took ten years to complete. Its role was to link Sydney with the agricultural lands of the Hunter Valley. This was important so that farm produce could be brought to the main centres of population. Sheep and cattle could be easily driven along the road, either to the farms or back to Sydney for slaughter. The need to connect Sydney with centres of agriculture was a strong push factor causing the colonial government to spend time and money on road-building.

Left: Convict-built stone embankment
Below: Convict-built road

What was Built?

Roads, bridges, wharves, quarries and high stone walls to stabilise the road were all constructed. Some of the stone walls are thirteen metres high, and the blocks can weigh over half a tonne each. The 240 kilometres of the Great North Road were all laid long before machinery and power tools were available.

Conservation

Before being listed as a World Heritage Site, parts of the Great North Road had been covered with highways and buildings. Some of the sections in remote bushland were under threat from decay, overgrowth and vandalism. In the 1990s, conservation groups banded together to help preserve the road. Government bodies added their assistance and, in 2010, UNESCO added the site to the World Heritage List.

Tourism

The Old Great North Road is now a long walking or cycling track. Cars are not permitted on it because of the damage they would cause.

Willandra Lakes

The Willandra Lakes in New South Wales are a series of ancient lakes that dried up about 18,000 years ago. The dry lakebeds and surrounding dunes are the site of fossil remains of giant wombats and kangaroos. There are also hundreds of fossilised human footprints made in clay, dating back 19,000 to 23,000 years ago, and human remains dating back to nearly 60,000 years ago. These ancient human bones are some of the oldest found anywhere on Earth, making Lake Mungo one of the world's most valuable archaeological sites. A cremation burial site in Lake Mungo has been dated to 40,000 years ago, making it the oldest ever discovered.

The sandy lakes have also revealed shell middens and stone tools preserved from the ancient past. The stone axes found at the Willandra Lakes were made from a stone that is not available in the area. Archaeologists assume that ancient people must have travelled long distances to trade stone items with other groups.

The traditional Aboriginal custodians of the area are the Paakantji, Ngiyampaa and Mutthi Mutthi people. They maintain a strong spiritual connection with the ancient remains and seek to ensure that any archaeological investigation into the skeletons of their ancestors is carried out respectfully.

The Willandra Lakes have been on the World Heritage List since 1981.

How the Site is Being Protected

- Grazing and watering of livestock is prohibited in some areas.
- Tourist access is also prohibited in some areas.
- A management committee for the area is made up of representatives of government bodies as well as Aboriginal traditional custodians.
- Feral rabbits and goats are controlled.
- Natural erosion is reduced where possible.

Greater Blue Mountains

How the Site is Being Protected

The Blue Mountains, just west of Sydney, have a reputation as a haunt for artists and conservationists. The beautiful towns throughout the mountains attract tourists for bushwalking in the summer and for the snow in the winter. The Winter Magic Festival is held each year to celebrate the winter solstice.

Jenolan Caves

Millions of years ago, before the whole area was lifted into mountains, the Jenolan Caves were once part of a seabed. Shell and coral fossils are found in the rocks of the caves, which are Australia's most remarkable limestone cave system.

The traditional owners of the land at Jenolan are the Wiradjuri and the Gundungurra peoples, while the caves are in the lands of the Burra Burra people, a clan group of the Gundungurra Nation. The caves, called Binoomea, were places of ceremonial importance and the cave pools were known for their healing properties.

Settlers discovered the caves in the early 1800s. The damage that some early tourists caused was halted in 1872 when breaking off pieces from the caves was made illegal. In the late 1880s, the Jenolan Caves increased in popularity as a tourist destination.

Exploration

The Blue Mountains were the first mountain range explored by settlers. Until they found a way to cross the Blue Mountains to the west of Sydney, they had no idea about the extensive plains suitable for pastures and crops, and large river systems for irrigation. The growing settlement needed more land, so Governor Macquarie encouraged explorers to find out what was over the mountains.

In 1813, Blaxland, Lawson and Wentworth discovered a way across them, allowing settlers to spread into the plains beyond. Aboriginal people had been crossing the Blue Mountains for generations, so the explorers used Aboriginal guides to lead the way. The exploration party followed the ridges of the hills, rather than descending into the valleys, where bushwalkers still lose their way in the dense forests.

Geology

The Blue Mountains are a part of the Great Dividing Range. They were formed by sedimentation, uplifting and twisting of the rock layers and erosion by rivers.

Three Sisters

The Three Sisters rock formation at Katoomba is one of Australia's most famous landmarks. An extensive infrastructure has been built to allow viewing from a large platform, and to cater for the needs of tourists and their vehicles. A number of local businesses depend on the Three Sisters for their livelihood.

World Heritage Site

The Greater Blue Mountains area has been a UNESCO Word Heritage Site since 2000. The vegetation is important for its connection to the ancient continent of Gondwana. The extensive variety of eucalypt trees is unique and the rare Wollemi pine is a relic from the age of the dinosaurs.

Lord Howe Island Group

These isolated volcanic islands were World Heritage listed for their landscapes and wildlife in 1992. They include Lord Howe Island, Admiralty Islands, Mutton Bird Islands and Ball's Pyramid. The islands are administered by the government of New South Wales.

Heritage features

- Most southerly coral reef in the world
- Outstanding landscapes
- Major breeding colony of the Providence Petrel
- Haven for threatened species such as the Lord Howe Woodhen
- Home to the largest stick insect in the world, the Lord Howe Island Phasmid
- Formed by an undersea volcano six million years ago
- Many examples of evolution in isolation
- Cloud forests on the mountain tops, a rarity amongst small Pacific Ocean islands

Threats to the World Heritage Site

- Development and clearing for buildings and agriculture
- Tourism
- Feral pigs, cats, rats, mice and goats
- Commercial fishing
- Weeds

Did You Know?
The Kentia Palm is the most popular garden and indoor palm tree in the world. It comes from Lord Howe Island.

Glossary

aesthetic	relating to beauty
dock	place where ships are repaired or built
forgery	creating a false document to gain some advantage
heritage	thing or characteristic that is handed down from previous generations
mess hall	dining room in an institution
silo	place to store large amounts of grain
shell middens	places where the debris from eating shellfish and other food has accumulated over time
species	separate group of animals or plants
transportation	sending convicts from Britain to the Australian colonies
unparalleled	exceptional and unique
UNESCO	United Nations Educational, Scientific and Cultural Organization

---

Index

Australian Institute of Architects 10
Cockatoo Island 22
heritage councils 10
Hyde Park Barracks 20
National Trust 10
Old Government House 19
Old Great North Road 24
plan of action 8
shipwrecks 10
Willandra Lakes 26

Visit these websites to find out more about Australia's World Heritage Sites and special places

whc.unesco.org/en/list
www.environment.gov.au/heritage